WESTMINSTER SCHOOLS

SMYTHE GAMBRELL
LIBRARY

PRESENTED BY

michael Lee
1986

Cate Candler

A New True Book

LANGUAGE

By Carol Greene

This "true book" was prepared
under the direction of
Illa Podendorf,
formerly with the Laboratory School,
University of Chicago

 CHILDRENS PRESS, CHICAGO

Road sign in New Delhi, India

*This book is for
Sandy and Jerry Cooper,
because they think language
is important.*

Library of Congress Cataloging in Publication Data

Greene, Carol.
    Language.

    (A New true book)
    Includes index.
    Summary: A brief introduction to language as communication, as a changing thing, as a complex family with 3000 members, and as a tool for both learning and having fun.
    1. Language and languages—Juvenile literature.
    [1. Language and languages] I. Title. II. Series.
    P124.G7 1983   400   83-7421
    ISBN 0-516-01694-6   AACR2

TABLE OF CONTENTS

WHO NEEDS LANGUAGE?

Who needs language?

To answer this question, try an experiment. You'll need a friend to help.

Try to work with your friend on a project without talking. You can't use any sounds. You can't speak any words and you can't write any words. You have to work without language.

How did it go? Did you end up laughing? Or did you end up angry? Did the project get done?

Who needs language? *You* do! We *all* do!

WHAT IS LANGUAGE?

What is language?

Language is what people speak and what people write.

It is the words used to name things and actions.

7

How could we tell
someone about an
elephant if we didn't have
the word *elephant*?

How could we tell
someone to run if we
didn't have the word *run*?

Coca-Cola is sold all over the world. The French product is at the left. The Arabic one is on the right.

Words are an important part of language. But they aren't the only part.

Have you ever heard someone speak a foreign language? Of course, the words are different. But so is the sound of the language.

The German sign (top left) points out water for dogs, Kentucky Fried Chicken is sold in France (top right), the movie *Absence of Malice* (below left) is shown in Spanish, and the signs in Hong Kong often include Chinese as well as English words (below right).

The French language sounds different from the Spanish language. German sounds different from Chinese.

So sound is an important part of language, too.

Another important part of language is the way words are put together.

In English you can't just say, "See cat the I." No one would know what you were talking about.

But everyone can understand you when you say, "I see the cat." You have put the words together in the right way. The last important part of language is grammar. Grammar is the rules that

Each language has rules. Everyone must learn these rules in order to write and speak their language correctly.

help make each language clear and easy to understand.

"Her don't want none of them mouses." is not a clear sentence. The grammar is wrong.

"She doesn't want any of those mice." is a clear sentence. The grammar is correct.

HOW DID LANGUAGE BEGIN?

How did language begin?
The answer is simple.
We don't know—at least
not exactly.

Some people who study
language think that long,
long ago people imitated
the sounds they heard
around them.

They heard a dog go
"bowwow." So when they
saw a dog, they said,

"Bowwow." Soon a dog was known as a bowwow.

Other people think those long-ago people made up sounds to go with actions.

When Mabel Caveperson wanted more firewood, she pointed to the woodpile and said, "Umf."

Marvin Caveperson learned
that when Mabel pointed
to the woodpile and said,
"Umf," he'd better get busy.

Soon Mabel didn't even
have to point. She just said,
"Umf," and Marvin got busy.

Other people have still
more ideas about how
language began. But no
matter how it did begin, it
must have made life much
easier for those early
people.

Can you read these picture signs? The long sign above tells you that you can find food, lavatories, showers, nursery, and telephone and telex facilities. The ones below say walk, stop, and duck crossing.

HOW DOES LANGUAGE CHANGE?

Language is not a dead thing. It doesn't stay the same forever.

Language is alive. And like all living things, it grows and changes.

Hundreds of years ago, English people said, "He sat him doun upon a stane." Today they say, "He sat down on a stone."

Children reading in Thailand

Language changes.

One way it changes is by borrowing words from other languages.

Kindergarten was once a German word. *Garage* started out as a French word. *Canyon* started out as a Spanish word.

In Ireland (above) road signs are written in English as well as Irish (Gaelic). Some signs ask people not to do silly things that will cause damage to property.

Now we think of them all as good English words. Sometimes people make up new words for new things. *Astronaut* is a word like that. So is *feedback*.

The increased use of microcomputers has added hundreds of new words to all languages.

People didn't need these words until they knew about electronics—or dreamed of traveling to the stars.

Sometimes new words start out as slang. People don't think they're very good words at first.

Hi started out as a slang word. Then more and more people used it all the time. Now *hi* is a perfectly good word.

Other new words start out as names of products. But after a while they can mean any product like the first one.

American-made soaps sold in France often combine English with French. Can you find the Ivory Snow soap?

Kleenex is the name of one brand of tissue. Now people use this word for any tissue.

Sometimes language changes just by the way it is spoken.

Often words are made
shorter. *TV* is easier to say
than "television." *Stereo* is
easier than "stereophonic
record and tape player."

Sometimes two words
are put together. "Do not"
becomes "don't." "We are"
becomes "we're." Words
like "don't" and "we're" are
called contractions.

Sometimes people even
change the rules of
grammar. They do this by

Deaf worker on an electronic assembly line in Japan receives "signing" instructions from a supervisor.

breaking them for a long time.

It used to be wrong to say "I will feed the fish." You were supposed to say "I *shall* feed the fish." But just about everyone says "I will" now.

A LOT OF LANGUAGES

Actually, language has
been changing ever since
it began. Some people
think there was just one
language to start with.
They believe all other
languages came from that
first language.

Today there are about
three thousand languages
spoken in the world. Some
are spoken by more
people than others. The

An Indian sign (left) warns people to guard against "shoe-lifters." Thailand has signs (above) in its own language as well as English.

most popular languages are Chinese, English, Hindustani, Spanish, Russian, German, Japanese, Indonesian, French, Italian, Portuguese, Arabic, and Bengali.

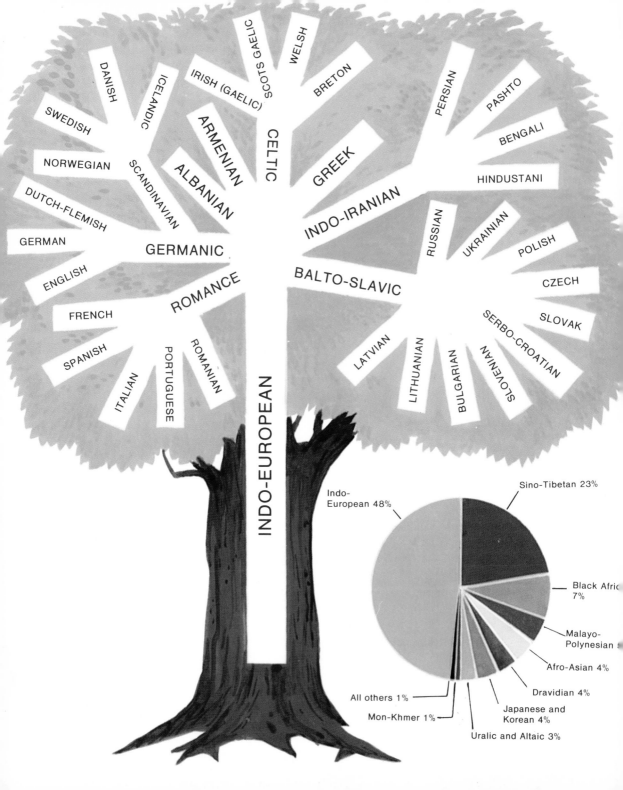

People who study languages have put them into families. They say that all the languages in one family come from a parent language.

The largest language family is called Indo-European. Half the people in the world speak languages in this family.

اتيث خج خ ذز ش ش ض ظ Arabic

АБВГДЕЖЗИКЛМ Cyrillic

אבגדהוזחטיכלמנ Hebrew

กขคฆงจฉฎ Thai

ΑΒΓΔΕαβγδε Greek

When written, many languages use their own alphabets.
You can see how the letters from different languages are different.

English belongs to the Indo-European language family. So do French, Spanish, German, and many other languages.

New Guinea (above left),
Brazil (above right), and Poland
(left). Each country has
its own language.

WHY NOT ONE LANGUAGE?

If everybody in the world
spoke just one language,
maybe they would get
along better.

31

Some people have invented languages for everyone in the world to use. Three of these languages are Volapük, Esperanto, and Interlingua.

But most people don't want to give up their own language. So we go on having a lot of languages.

VOLAPÜK: O Fat obas, kel binol in süls, paisaludomöz nem ola! Kömomöd monargän ola! Jenomöz vil olik, äs in sül, i su tal!

ESPERANTO: Patro nia, kiu estas en la ĉielo, sankta estu via nomo; venu regeco via; estu volo via, kiel en la ĉielo, tiel ankaŭ sur la tero.

INTERLINGUA: Nostre Patre qui es in le celos, que tu nomine sia sanctificate; que tu regno veni; que tu voluntate sia facite como in celo assi etiam in terra.

The first part of the Lord's Prayer written in three languages—Volapük, Esperanto, and Interlingua.

MAKING
LANGUAGE WORK

Language is one of the most important tools we have. But it is like any other tool. We must learn to use it properly before it will work for us.

A hammer is no good if we don't know how to use it. But once we learn how to use a hammer, we can pound nails with it.

Once we learn how to use language, we can tell people what we are thinking and feeling. We can understand what they tell us.

We can tell and understand even more when we learn a foreign language. We learn to say words and sentences in that language. But we also learn about the lives of the people who speak that language.

If we study Spanish, we learn the word *fiesta*. It means "feast" or "party."

Spanish (above) and Greek (left) signs.

But we also learn about
the kinds of parties
Spanish-speaking people
have. We might even get
to go to one. That's the
best way of all to learn.

38

HAVING FUN
WITH LANGUAGE

Language isn't all work. Sometimes it can be a lot of fun.

We can use language to write poems. Poems can tell how something beautiful or funny or scary or sad makes us feel.

What is the most beautiful thing you've ever seen? Write a poem about it.

What's the funniest thing
you can think of? A
hippopotamus in a baby
buggy? Write a poem
about it.

We can use language to make up jokes, too.

"Knock knock."

"Who's there?"

"Orange."

"Orange who?"

"Orange you getting tired of knock-knock jokes?"

That joke is funny because you can make the word *orange* sound like the word *aren't.* It's funny because of language. Can you make up a knock-knock joke?

We can even use language to make up whole worlds. We can invent a land and give it a name. We can invent the people who live there. We can make up stories about what they do.

What kind of land would you invent? What would you call it?

Language is important. It's work and it's fun. Best of all, it's yours. Use it well!

WORDS YOU SHOULD KNOW

borrowing(BAR • oh • ing) — taking from something else, especially taking a word or phrase from one language and using it in another language

brand name(BRAND NAIM) — a trade name used to identify a specific product, *Coca-Cola* is an example

change(CHAINJ) — to make or become different

contractions(kun • TRAK • shunz) — words that have been shortened — I'm, you're, and they're are examples

electronics(eh • lek • TRON • ix) — a branch of physics that deals with the movement and use of electrons and how machines can use electrons

experiment(ex • PEER • ah • mint) — test; a method to try out an idea

family(FAM • ih • lee) — a group related by common characteristics

grammar(GRAM • er) — the study of words, their different forms, and how they are used in relationship with other words

imitate(im • ih • tait) — to copy; to follow

invented(in • VEN • tid) — made up or thought up for the first time

parent language(PAIR • ent • LANG • wij) — the source from which other languages developed

project(PRAH • jekt) — a planned task or job often done by students

slang(SLANG) — an informal use of a word, often introduced into a language; a change in a word's meaning

About the Author

Carol Greene has written over 30 books for children, plus stories, poems, songs, and filmstrips. She has also worked as a children's editor and a teacher of writing for children. She received a B.A. in English Literature from Park College, Parkville, Missouri, and an M.A. in Musicology from Indiana University. Ms. Greene lives in St. Louis, Missouri. When she isn't writing she likes to read, travel, sing, do volunteer work at her church—and write some more. Her The Super Snoops and the Missing Sleepers *and* Sandra Day O'Connor, First Woman on the Supreme Court *have also been published by Childrens Press.*

INDEX